Preserving Our Culture

Preserving Our Culture:

The Joy of Jamaican Ring Games and More!

Christopher C. Murray and Thrica A. Rookwood
Illustrator Owen Harris

XULON PRESS

Xulon Press
2301 Lucien Way #415
Maitland, FL 32751
407.339.4217
www.xulonpress.com

Xulon
PRESS

Printed in the United States of America.
Edited by Xulon Press.

ISBN-13: 9781545621899

Table of Contents

Acknowledgment

It is a delight to express our gratitude to Mr. Owen Harris, the art illustrator, who so well ably demonstrated the ring games in an artistic manner.

Also thank you to Mrs. Georgia Murray and Mr. Stanley Rookwood, wife and husband of Christopher C. Murray and Thrica Rookwood, for their unfeigned support and understanding to finish this project.

Professor Fitzroy J. Henry: thank you for your most valuable contribution on obesity and the Caribbean.

Introduction

Heritage is as important as future goals and aspirations. It has been said on several occasions that if someone forgets where they are coming from, its highly likely they may not reach where they are going. The fruit of a tree must never be held at a greater position than the roots from which it came, for it is the root that determines the fruit.

Subsequently, we desire to propel all our readers on a journey that will be educational for some and a grand reminder for others. This journey will carry us back in time to revisit our roots.

Growing up in the land of wood and water, Jamaica, the memories as a child are treasured and of great delight when mentioned. Memories of forging relationships with schoolmates and neighborhood children while playing games that made us laugh unendingly, tired beyond bathing, and healthy beyond constant medication.

At night, we were summoned by our parents beckoning call to "come inside." Although it was dark, that was of no challenge to us, as we were all lost in a ring game that had us running, skipping, shouting, and dancing. Please take special note that were called "inside," as this will become an important point later.

At school, the games had a mixture of children, no one was too good or too bad or too poor or too rich not to play. As a matter of fact, for some of the games, the more the merrier. Going to school was a delight; although for some of us, school meant before lessons began in the morning, break time, and lunchtime only. Before classes began, we had already worked a full day's job by the appearance of our soaked uniforms, but by the time break and lunchtime came around, we were ready again.

"Depression" was an unknown word to us, not to mention insomnia, of which some of us still perhaps don't know that word. After a "hard" day at school and more "hard work" in somebody's yard, when bedtime came, we would say in Jamaica, "As you say who dat," we were fast asleep. No time to stay up all night on a vibrating gadget, with a book for faces, or a tweeting bird sending constant messages, or snapping chats with abbreviated messages. Sleep was too sweet to miss.

As we observe the children today constantly glued to a handheld machine while tiptoeing with their fingers continuously, smiling without a joke being heard, dancing without an audible sound for others to hear, not breaking a sweat, but tired most of the times, but not sleeping because of the ongoing night shifts of communication, it goes without saying they are being robbed of treasured experiences by always being stationed before a television box, a video game, or the famous smart phones, searching for amusement or entertainment.

While we had to be called to come inside, today's children are being told to go outside! From a psychological standpoint, this generation has been classified as the loneliest generation with so many "likes", so many "friend requests" that make them connected, yet so disconnected. Friendships can end by simply clicking a "block" button. People send smiley faces while not smiling, or say "LOL," but are silent in their rooms, or sending beautiful hearts while having a broken heart—no wonder they can't sleep at night.

It is a travesty and something must be done. Hence, this book, we hope, will be a reminder to parents to spend some time teaching their children and the children in their communities and teachers to set aside a few minutes to teach their classes what fun used to be, which was being socially interactive without a phone in between. Or what "LOL" truly looks and sounds like.

Are you ready? There's a brown girl in the ring

1, 2, 3, red light

Let's go!

Dandy Shandy (Dodge ball, sittings)

Game Instructions

This game is played with two persons standing at opposite ends while five to twelve children are standing in the middle.

The two persons standing at either end will throw a tennis size ball or box folded as a ball over the heads of the children standing in the middle.

After about two throws overhead, the two persons will start aiming to hit the persons in the middle. body that's hit loses his or her place in the game. The task of those in the middle is to "dodge" the ball as much as they can. The person left in the middle is considered the winner.

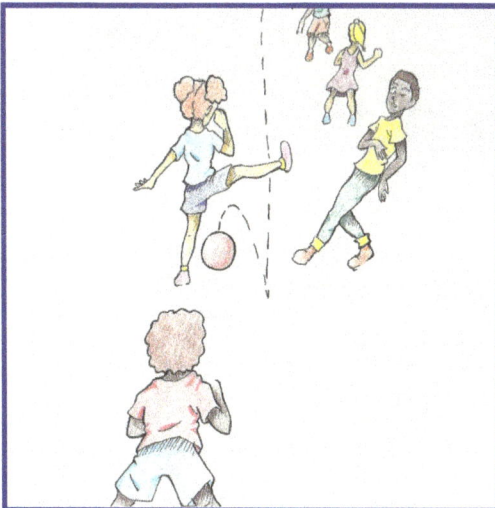

Simon Says

Game Instructions

This game is played by giving several commands and the persons must only respond to the command that says, "Simon says." Commands such as, "Simon says, 'Jump', 'clap', 'dance', 'skip', and 'laugh.'"

If a command is given without saying, "Simon says," and persons respond by doing the actions, such person will lose their place in the game. The last person left will be considered the winner. This game can be played with many persons.

Simon Says ring game.

How Many Steps to the Queen?

Game Instructions

This game is played with ten to twenty children standing in a horizontal line about forty feet away from one child who stands at the front, considered "the queen."

The participants will ask, "How many steps to meet the queen?"

The queen will respond by saying, "One to three giant steps," or, "One to three frog leaps," or, "One to three baby steps," or, "One to three scissor cuts."

The participants will ask, "May I?"

Without saying "May I," the movements cannot be taken. When the queen turns around after saying, "Yes, you may," if he or she catches anyone moving, such individuals will be sent back to the starting line. The participant that reaches the queen first will be the winner.

How many Steps to the Queen ring game

1,2,3, Red light

Game Instructions

This game is played with ten or more children all standing in a horizontal line at a distance facing one child at the front. The child at the front turns his or her back to the group.

The child standing at the front shouts, "One, two, three, red light!" and quickly turns around. The group of children will aim to reach the child standing at the front without being caught moving. Whosoever is caught moving will lose their place in the game.

Bruk Rock Stone (Go dung a Manuel Road)

Game Instructions

This is another entertaining, exciting, and enjoyable game that, once learned, children can't get enough of it. It can be played with up to ten players, but requires a high level of concentration so no one gets hurt.

This game is usually played on a smooth surface. The children are required to sit/kneel in a circle with each student having a stone in his or her hand. Once the song begins, each child will pass their stone in a clockwise direction in front of the child beside them. The children are required to keep the rhythm. If a child falls behind on the rhythm, that child is considered out. Each player is expected to move as quickly and cautiously as possible to prevent the stones from piling up or avoid getting their fingers smashed. The game tempo never changes.

Lyrics

Go dung a Manuel Road, gal an bwoy,
Fe go bruk rock stone, gal an bwoy.
Go dung a Manuel Road, gal an bwoy,

Fe go bruk rock stone, gal an bwoy.

Bruk dem one by one, *gal an bwoy,*

Bruk dem two by two, *gal an bwoy,*

Bruk dem three by three, *gal an bwoy,*

Bruk dem Four by Four, *gal an bwoy,*

Finga mash, no cry, *gal an bwoy,*

Memba a play we a play, *gal an bwoy.*

Bruk Dem One By One ring game

"Here Comes Nancy on Her Pony" Instructions

Game Instructions

The students will form a circle and in the middle of the circle is a child representing Nancy on her pony. As the song begins, the children will clap in unison to a single beat while the child in the middle skips around. When they get to the line, "Back to back to back my baby," the children pair up and will all jump and spin around with their backs facing their partner. At the line, "side to side to side my baby," the partners will face sideways, then forward.

At the end, they can repeat the song as many times as they want.

Lyrics

Here comes Nancy on here pony, riding on our big fat pony.
Here comes Nancy on her pony and this is what she told me...
Back to back to back my baby,
Side to side to side my baby,
Front to front to front my baby
And this is what they told me.
(Repeat)

Little Miss Nancy Went to Town

Game Instructions

This is another game that children love to play. I must hasten to say that the intent of the game must never be taken as discrimination or insulting, but instead for fun, relaxation, and laughter. It can be played inside or outside, in a clear space for the children to form a reasonable sized circle. In the circle, a child will skip around, as the persons holding the circle will sing the song. The child in the middle is expected to do the actions of the song at the appropriate time. For example, when it gets to the line, "When she see a ugly girl she cut her eye and pass her," She will choose a child randomly and "cut" her eye at that child. As soon as it gets to the next line, "When she see a pretty girl she take her hand and call her," she will use her finger to call a student of choice and by the end of the song, that child becomes Miss Nancy. This game is repeated as often as the children choose to play.

Lyrics

Little Miss Nancy went to town, went to town, went to town.

Little Miss Nancy went to town to buy a pack of needle.

When she see a ugly girl, a ugly girl, a ugly girl,

when she see a ugly girl, she cut her eye and pass her.

When she see a pretty girl, a pretty girl, a pretty girl,

when she see a pretty girl, she take her hand and call her.

That's the way my money goes, my money goes, my money goes

That's the way my money goes to buy a pack of needle.

What can you do Punchinello little fella?

Game Instructions

This game, like all the other ring games, can be played with five to ten players. All the children hold hands and surround one child who stands in the center of the ring. The children then sing the Punchinello Little Fella song, which goes, "What can you do Punchinello little fella?" With each line, the child in the middle of the ring dances. The children forming the circle have to imitate his or her moves. The children then decide who will go next and the game continues with children singing as they change places.

Lyrics

Who's coming next Punchinello?
Who's coming next Punchinello?
Who's coming next Punchinello?

What can you do Punchinello?
What can you do Punchinello?
What can you do Punchinello?

We can do it too Punchinello.
We can do it too Punchinello.
We can do it too Punchinello.

Brown Girl in the Ring

Game Instructions

A group of ten to fifteen players form a circle. Then they sing the song and clap to a rhythm. One child goes in the center of the circle. During the first verse, that child dances inside the circle. On the second verse, starting with, "Show me your motion," the child shows her moves! On the third verse, the child chooses a partner with whom to skip around inside the ring. At the end of the song, that chosen partner becomes the next "brown girl in the ring" and the song starts over again.

Lyrics

There's a brown girl in the ring, tra la la la la
There's a brown girl in the ring, tra la la la la la
Brown girl in the ring, tra la la la la
She looks like a sugar and a plum*
Plum, plum!

Then you show me your motion, tra la la la la
Then you show me your motion, tra la la la la la

Show me your motion, tra la la la la
She looks like a sugar and a plum*
Plum, plum!
Then you skip and take a partner, tra la la la la
Skip and take a partner, tra la la la la la
Skip and take a partner, tra la la la la
She looks like a sugar and a plum*
Plum, plum!

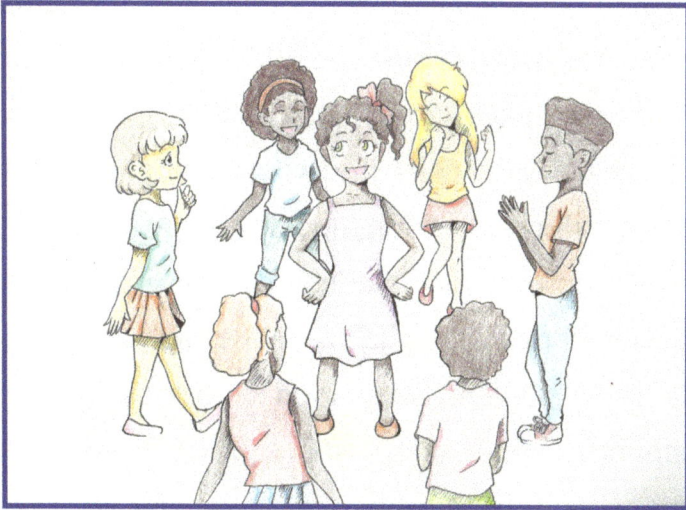

Brown Girl in the Ring ring game

Dog and Bone

Game Instructions

Dog and Bone is a game that is played with two teams standing facing each other in a vertical line. Both teams should stand equidistant away from the bone in the middle on either side. The Bone could be a small stick that looks like a baton on a block or a stone, or a stone on a small table, or whatever is available. One person, who is considered the caller, will stand to the side and quickly call, "Dog and Bone."

Once the caller calls, the two persons at the front of the line will race to fetch the bone in the middle. The person who reaches the bone first will grab the bone and race back to their team, while the other person will try to prevent the person with the bone from reaching safety. If the person with the bone reaches home without been hit by the other team, their team gets one point, but if the person without the bone hits the one with the bone, that team gets the point.

Once the teams are back home, the players will join the line at the back and the persons at the front become the next player to fetch the bone. The cycle will continue until all the players get a turn. At the end, the team with the most points wins the game.

Dog and Bone ring game.

Bull in a Pen

Game Instructions

This is a rough, but exciting game that is loved by children and adults in Jamaica. This game is played with at least eight children forming a circle and one child stands in the middle. Before the game begins, the child in the middle will walk around and ask "What kind of pen is this?" and the partners, after agreeing, will respond by saying, "Iron pen, rubber pen, wooden pen," or another kind of pen, which will vary based on the children's creativity.

After the naming of the pens, the group will chant, "Bull in a pen can come out" to a rhythm then the person in the middle will choose the pen that he or she thinks will allow then to escape. If the try is unfruitful, the child will return to the middle and try another pen. This will continue until the child escapes the circle. Once the bull escapes, all the children in the circle will chase the child, who's considered the "bull," until he is caught. The first child to catch the bull becomes the next bull and the game continues until they all get a chance to be the bull.

Lyrics

Bull in a pen, can come out

Bull in a pen, can come out

What kind of pen is this? Iron Pen

What kind of pen is this? Iron Pen

Bull in a pen, can come out

Bull in a pen, can come out

What kind of pen is this? Scissor Pen

What kind of pen is this? Scissor Pen

Bull in a pen, can come out

Bull in a pen, can come out

What kind of pen is this? Wood Pen

What kind of pen is this? Wood Pen

(N.B. The names of the pen vary based on the creativity of the children)

Bull in a Pen ring game.

Blue Bird, Blue Bird in and out of the window

Game Instructions

Students stand in a circle with arms raised and palms of hands pressing on neighbors' hands to form windows. One person is selected to be the Bluebird. He or she will walk through the hands of the children that represent the windows as the song is sung, and stops at the closest person on the word "tired." When the student stops behind the child, he will pat him on the shoulder. At the end, that child will joint the first Bluebird to make it two Bluebirds. Both of them will again go through the windows singing the song from the beginning. This process will continue with the line of birds getting longer and longer until the there's only one person to hold the window and then the game begins again. Repeat as often as necessary.

Lyrics

Bluebird, bluebird, in and out of the window.
Bluebird, bluebird, in and out of the window.
Bluebird, bluebird, in and out of the window.
Oh Johnny, I'm tired.

Take a little girl and tap her on the shoulder
Take a little girl and tap her on the shoulder
Take a little girl and tap her on the shoulder
Oh Johnny, I'm tired.

Those Born in January, Skip Around

Game Instructions

"Those Born in January" is another fun game that can be played inside or outside with as many children as possible. This game is often used as a means of reinforcing the months of the year at the infant level in most Jamaican schools. The children are expected to form a large circle without holding hands. As they stand in the circle, the children will begin singing the song "Those born in January, skip around" and clapping to a beat while the children born in the respective months will respond accordingly. Once their month is called, the child or children will skip to the middle of the circle and keep going until the next month is called. As soon as they rejoin the circle, those born in the next month will skip to the middle of the circle and the cycle continues until they get to December.

Lyrics

Those born in January, skip around.
Those born in January, skip around.
Tra la la la la la, Tra, la, la, la, la, la
Those born in January, skip around.

Those born in February, skip around.

Those born in, February skip around.

Tra la la la la la, Tra, la, la, la, la, la

Those born in February, skip around.

(Repeat with every month of the year)

Hide and Seek

Game Instructions

Hide and Seek is another fun game that children of every nationality love to play. Like most games, there is no specific number of children that can participate in this game. However, to begin the game, one child covers their face/eyes and counts to ten while the other players run to hide somewhere. At the end of the count, the counter yells, "Ready or not, here I come!" Once the children hiding hear that sound, they know they need to remain as quiet as possible so they won't be caught.

The child who is the seeker will try to find all the children as quickly as possible. The last child to be found becomes the seeker in the next game. This game can continue for long as the kids want, or until all the children get a turn.

Chinese Telephone

Game Instructions

Chinese Telephone is a simple game that is used to establish how information can become distorted after passing through secondary mediums. Adults and children can play this game. It can be used as an ice-breaker or to cement a point. This game can be played with a small number of persons or a large group. The participants (children or adult) are required to form a circle or a line. The persons at the front of the line will think of a message and pass it on to the next person. The cycle will continue until the message reaches the last person who is required to say what he or she heard and is then compared to the first message that was sent. During the passing of the message, if the receiver did not hear the message, the child telling is not allowed to repeat. Whatever the receiver hears is what he/she will have to pass on to the next person. Usually, that's what makes the game hilarious. The amusing thing about this game is that usually the last person never says the message correctly. It is fun to hear the message all scrambled up.

Hopscotch

Game Instructions

This game only requires a piece of chalk and a surface or stick and a dirt surface outside to draw the squares. The boxes would look like the one seen in the picture below, which would be three single square joined together vertically, another two squares joined horizontally followed by a single, then another double and finally a single square: a total of nine squares.

Once they are finish drawing the squares, the first player is selected by toasting a coin or saying, "Eeny, meeny, miny, moe." The player then throws a stone inside the first square and then hops over the first one and into all the other squares except the first one and back. On your way back, you are required to pick up the stone using one hand without falling before jumping on all the squares. The same procedure continues with the player throwing the stone or what we call "man" in the second square while the player jumps in square one, three, and onward. Never jump in the square that has the stone or "man."

Player one continues to play until he is out by his foot touching the line, he jumps into the box with a stone, or he/she misses the correct box that they should throw the "man" or stone in. Once this player is out, another player has a chance to throw. Now this player has to skip two boxes at all times, his and the previous player's box. This continues until all players gets a turn or someone wins the game by successfully throwing the "man" or stone into all the boxes.

Hopscotch

Musical Chairs

Game Instructions

Musical Chairs is another fun game that is usually full of excitement and keeps the adrenaline rush going. As the name suggests, it is played to some kind of music, preferably an up-tempo beat or to the sound of a tambourine. This will create a festive environment, encouraging the players to have fun. You can use the same song repeatedly or you could have a list of songs from which to choose because the game could go for a long time, depending on the skillfulness of the players.

To begin playing this game, assign someone to be in charge of the music whose sole responsibility is to start and stop the music. Once this person is in place, secure a wide-open space, whether inside or outside. This place should be free of obstacles to avoid any form of injuries. The next thing is to set up the chairs in a circle or in a line. If the chairs are in a line, they are placed inside out. This means that one chair is facing the left while the other is facing the right and it follows that order until all the chairs are lined up. It is important to note, you should always have one chair less than the amount of persons playing. For example, if there are ten players, there should be nine chairs. If you don't have chairs, use whatever is available to you.

After few minutes or seconds of playing the song, the teacher or host should stop the music. When the music stops, each player needs to sit in a chair. The player that did not find a chair is the one that is out. Once the player leaves, the host or the other players need to remove a chair before playing the next round. This procedure continues until the last two players are left with one chair. The music will play again and as soon as it stops, the player sitting on the chair is the winner.

If the chairs are place in a circle, all the rules explained above apply.

The Farmer in the Dell

Game Instructions

The Farmer in the Dell is a famous game among children that replicates well the true epitome of what family should be. In this ring game, the children will form a circle with a player in the middle. The player will skip around as other children sing the song. The farmer then chooses a wife to join him in the center. If the farmer is a girl, she will choose a husband and not a wife. As the game go on, the wife will choose a child from the circle to join her in the center. This process will continue until it gets to the cheese. The children all clap hands as they sing this last verse, gathering around the cheese. The cheese will stand alone in the middle as she looks for an escape route. At the end of the song, all the children will rush down on the child to take a bite if he or she is not able to elude the group.

Lyrics

The farmer in the dell
The farmer in the dell
Hi ho the dairy o
The farmer in the dell

The farmer takes a wife
The farmer takes a wife
Hi ho the dairy o
The farmer takes a wife

The wife takes a child
The wife takes a child
Hi ho the dairy o
The wife takes a child

The child takes a nurse
The child takes a nurse
Hi ho the dairy o
The child takes a nurse

The nurse takes a dog
The nurse takes a dog
Hi ho the dairy o
The nurse takes a dog

The dog wants a cat
The dog wants a cat
Hi ho the dairy o
The dog wants a cat

The cat wants a mouse
The cat wants a mouse

Hi ho the dairy o

The cat wants a mouse

The mouse wants some cheese

The mouse wants some cheese

Hi ho the dairy o

The mouse wants some cheese

The cheese stands still

The cheese stands still

Hi ho the dairy o

The cheese stands still

Farmer in a Dell ring game

Esau and Jacob (Esau yes Jacob (Blind Man)

Game Instructions

Esau, Esau is another game that requires a high level of concentration and silence. This is so because the listener, who is blindfolded, will have to escape the caller by listening to the sound as he or she calls repeatedly. This game is played with two persons at a time. Both must be blindfolded and placed at separate ends of the room. One person is called "Esau" and the other is called "Jacob." Jacob is the caller/chaser and Esau is the responder/runner. The caller (Jacob) will call "Esau, Esau," and Esau will reply, "Yes Jacob!" As Jacob calls, Esau will listen to the sound and try to run away, while Jacob will listen to the sound and try to catch Esau. They will continue to call until they catch each other.

At the end, the game can start over with two other persons or the one caught could be replaced. The cycle can continue for as long as you want or until all persons present get a turn.

Marble Games

Game Instructions

This is definitely an outdoor game that is usually played by boys on a clear dirt surface. Boys are generally excited about a game of marble regardless of how humid the day was. All the money they had was invested in more marbles, especially a "zombie," which is the huge marble as this was seen as the master soldier that could take out several enemies at any one time.

This game can be played with up to three players at any time. To begin playing this game, draw a circle with a horizontal line about half a foot below and a second horizontal line about two meters away from the first line. After that, each player decides how many marbles they will put in the circle. Once that is decided, each player stands behind the line immediately after the circle and throws their marble to the next line. The marble closet to the line is the person who gets to play first. Each player will aim for the marbles in the circle to see how many they can hit out of the circle. If they hit any of the marbles on their way up, they keep playing until they miss. Once they miss, the next player gets a turn and the cycle continues. As the players hit the marbles out of the circle, those marbles belong to him. At the end of the game, the player with the most marble wins. The game can continue as long as each person has marbles.

S-T-O-P

Game Instructions

Another entertaining game for children is S-T-O-P. This game can be played with up to ten players standing in a circle. While in the circle, arms must be comfortably stretched out. Each child/player should lay his or her right hand on the upturned palm of the child to their right while using their left hand to cushion the right hand of the next person.

While spelling "s-t-o-p" each child uses his or her right hand to hit the hand of the child on their left at the mention of each letter. It will end up in a chain reaction. Naturally, it doesn't go around spelling "stop." After you spell the word, the next child in line to receive a hand slap (B) will be out if the child whose turn to do the hitting (A) can successfully make a hit.

This is where the fun is because child B can move his palm to dodge the hit; the only restriction is that child B's hand must rest on child A's left palm. We used to disallow child A from faking a hit and child B could only dodge around three times before being out. If child A misses three times, they're out, and if child B gets hit, then they're out.

Children, Children

<u>Lyrics</u>

Caller: Children, children

Responders: Yes mama!

Caller: Where have you been?

Responders: Grandpapa

Caller: What did he give you?

Responders: Bun and cheese

Caller: Where is my share?

Responders: Up in the air.

Caller: How can I reach it?

Responders: Climb on a broken chair.

Caller: Suppose I fall?

Responders: I don't care.

Caller: Who taught you those dirty manners?

Responders: The dog.

Caller: Who is the dog?

Responders: You!

Game Instructions

"Children, children" is not a ring game, but it is another fun game that requires no materials to play. Playing this game requires a lot of energy, as children will be running for a while, especially if they are athletic. Those children who are not athletic will likely be caught first.

To play this game, one child must be given the role of the caller. This child's responsibility is to act as the mother and call the children who are considered the responders in this case. The other children will respond to the questions asked by mother.

At the end of the responses, the children will run in several directions and the caller will chase them. The person who is caught first will become the next caller and the game can continue as long as you have the time.

Skip to My Lou

Game Instructions

Another entertaining game is "Skip to My Lou." This is a ring game that can be played with any number of children, both male and female. To play this game, first form a huge circle. Each child in the circle must have a partner, males and females. After the partners are selected, one child without a partner will stand in the middle of the circle. Players will choose which verse they want to sing when it's their turn, or they can make up new ones.

To the tune of "Skip, skip, skip to my Lou" the pairs will begin skipping around the circle. The child without a partner will skip around with the intention of stealing an appropriate partner. If the child was successful, the new partner will try to skip back to their original position without being touched by the chasing partner. Once they reach home, the chasing partner will return to the circle and start the new game. However, if the chasing partner catches them, the child who stole the partner will have to return him or her to the rightful owner.

The boy/girl on the next round who is without a partner then steals another partner. The person without the partner is the one who chooses which verse everyone will sing next.

Lyrics (Chorus)
Skip, skip, skip to my Lou,
Skip, skip, skip to my Lou,
Skip, skip, skip to my Lou,
Skip to my Lou, my darling.

Lost my partner, what shall I do?
Lost my partner, what shall I do?
Lost my partner, what shall I do?
Skip to my Lou, my darling.

I'll find another one, prettier, too.
I'll find another one, prettier, too.
I'll find another one, prettier, too.
Skip to my Lou, my darlin!

Can't get a red bird, blue bird'll do.
Can't get a red bird, blue bird'll do.

Can't get a red bird, blue bird'll do.
Skip to my Lou, my darlin!

Flies in the sugar bowl, shoo, shoo, shoo.
Flies in the sugar bowl, shoo, shoo, shoo.
Flies in the sugar bowl, shoo, shoo, shoo.
Skip to my Lou, my darlin!

1, 2, 3 Auntie Loulou

Game Instructions

Auntie Loulou is a skipping game that is played with a six-foot rope and two persons at both ends of the rope turning it. This game requires skills, concentration, and good timing. Once the game begins, all the children are expected to sing while the person in the middle of the rope is expected to have a high level of concentration in order to catch back the rope without losing the rhythm.

The children at both ends will spin the rope at a moderate pace while the child in the middle is expected to skip and try not to get out. The participants will chant the song as loud as possible while the child in the middle is skipping to the tune. For each number you say, the child will skip once. As soon as we get to Auntie Loulou, the child will stoop down, while the other children spinning the rope will raise their hands and spin it over his or her head once then the skipper and the persons holding the rope will try to synchronize again for the next three numbers. The process continues until they reach number ten. At ten, the child will skip once, then stoop while the children raise the rope and spin once. Repeat twice. After doing that, if the skipper doesn't get out, the game continues, starting at one until that child is out another child will get a turn.

The aim of the game is to see who can go the longest without getting out. It keeps all players on the edge of their seat, hoping and praying that nothing goes wrong when it is their turn. Children and adults alike can play this game.

Ring Around the Rosy

Lyrics

Ring around the rosy
Pocket full of posies
Ashes, ashes
We all fall down

Game Instructions

This game can be played both inside and out-side with four to six players. The aim of this game is to see who can remain in a frozen position for the longest time.

To play this game, all the children will form a circle and hold hands. While holding hands, they will decide if they will skip to the right or to the left first. Then, they will begin singing the song and skipping to the left or right. When they get to the line, "they all fall down", all the children will stoop down in the circle and begin to stir like stirring a pot as they sing, "Ashes in the water, ashes in the sea". The other two lines tell exactly what the next action are going to be as the children will all jump up and then freeze in position. The last person to become unfrozen is the winner! This game can be played for as long as time allows.

Queen Elizabeth

Lyrics

Queen Elizabeth, she died last night

She died with a fever, she died with a cold

She died with money like fifty cents

So what ya going to do?

Just throw it away!

She got brown eyes, she got lipstick

She got waist stand

A diggy dang, diggy dang, in dey

A diggy dang, diggy dang, in out dey

A diggy dang, diggy dang, side dey

A diggy dang, diggy dang, side dey

In dey, out dey, side dey, side dey

FREEZE!

Game Instructions

Queen Elizabeth requires concentration and eye hand coordination. This game can be played with any number of students, but it is more fun and easier to monitor if it's a smaller number.

To begin playing this game, children are asked to form a circle. Each person's left hand should be stretched out, palm up, while the right hand is stretched out, palm down. The game then continues with a simultaneous movement of each hand: the right hand slaps down on the neighboring hand while the left hand receives a similar slap. Thereafter, both hands turn horizontal and meet palm-to-palm on both sides and then each individual claps their own hands. This process continues until the song reaches, "she throw it away." After that, each player exhibits an attitude by placing their left hand on their hips and say the second verse of the game, and use the right hand and point to their eyes while mentioning "brown eyes" and then pretend to place lipstick on their lips.

Each player will then move according to the song by placing each hand on their hips, then jumping into the ring and shaking, then jumping out of the ring and shaking, and the players will then jump to either sides. Upon reaching the part of the song that says, "Freeze," each player will shout that word and all will remain frozen. If anyone laughs, winks, or shows any other type of movement, they will lose their part in the game. Ultimately, the winner is the last person left frozen at the end.

London Bridge

London Bridge is falling down,
Falling down, falling down
London Bridge is falling down,
Falling down, falling down
My fair lady

Send for the broom to sweep out the house
Sweep out the house, sweep out the house
Send for the broom to sweep out the house
Sweep the house, sweep out the house
My fair lady

Send for the map to wipe out the house
Wipe out the house, wipe out the house
Wipe out the house, wipe out the house
Send for the map to wipe out the house
My fair lady

Game Instructions

There is no specific number of children that are
required to play this game and it can be both an indoor
and outdoor game. The game is not limited to only the
two verses, but individuals can be as creative as pos-
sible and improvise by adding other verses.

This game is played with two children extending their hands toward each other while touching palms in an arch-shaped manner. Children will walk in a line holding each other's shoulders, while going in and out of the arch-held hands. While doing that, the children will be singing, upon reaching the part of the song that says, "Send for the map, wipe out the house", the arch-held hands will descend to try to capture one of the children. Whoever is caught will have to leave the game. The game will continue until one person is left and then becomes the winner.

London Bridge

Obesity, a growing problem

A major problem of Obesity – my fond memories of playing outside

Obesity is a complex problem and requires a multifaceted solution-based approach. It is most recognizable that there is an ongoing problem in the Caribbean. Mr. Fitzroy J. Henry from the College of Health Sciences, University of Technology states:

> The silent escalating epidemic of <u>obesity</u> is the underlying cause of most deaths in the Caribbean. If action is not taken to curb our increasingly <u>overweight</u> populations the resultant burden of chronic diseases will overwhelm our

health systems and ultimately retard our overall health and economic development. (Henry 2016)

Also, according to the **Minister of Health in Jamaica, Dr. Christopher Tufton**:

The obesity levels among young people in Jamaica are alarming. It is almost inevitable at this rate that persons will not only develop unhealthy habits, but the public-health system is going to be challenged, Those affected by obesity, the minister reasoned, will have challenges to live healthy lives, and the issue of unhealthy diets cannot be ignored, hence the need for a "more constructive conversation.

He continued: *"The issue has long-term negative impact not only on the health system, but the economy."* Therefore, it goes without saying that the issue of obesity is an unavoidable avoidable problem that steers stares not just Jamaica, but the entire Caribbean in the face. Mr. Fitzroy Henry cited in his research that it is a Caribbean problem that requires immediate holistic attention. Mr. Henry said, "***Most striking, is that during the last few decades obesity has risen to epidemic proportions in the Caribbean.***"

He continued to state:

*The dramatic shift in early childhood nutritional status over a ten year period is revealed in **Figure 1 (seen below)**. The decline in under-nutrition is notable with most Caribbean countries now having less than 4% children under-nourished. The remarkable finding is the rapid increase in overweight and obesity where rates changed from 6% to 14% during one decade. Although the global prevalence of overweight amongst pre-school children is estimated at 3.3%, these data showed that **Caribbean children are much higher than the global average**. Even more worrisome is the*

observation that the risk of adult obe-
sity is 2.0-2.6 times greater in obese
pre-school children than in non-obese
pre-school children.

Figure 1: Change (%) in under nutrition and obesity of children (0-5 years) in the Caribbean 2000-2010, Source: Caribbean Food and Nutrition Institute, 2011

This book attempts to profile one of the solutions for this problem. When we were growing up, whether at home or at school, our games were never tied to a computer or a phone, but the remedies were the sun, cool breeze, friends, running, jumping, and dancing. "We were soaked in sweat from being so active something more and more children are not experiencing on a daily basis.. We had fun laughing, loosing, or winning. We exercised without a gym or without a trainer. It was scarce that you would see an overweight child to the extent if one was seen unfortunately another problem would arisewhich was bullying. However, we are not addressing bullying now, but memories are sealed in our minds of laughing so loud and long about someone who got caught moving after hearing one two three red light, or a boy was in the ring dancing to the song, "Brown girl in the ring, tra la la la!"

Can't forget "bat up and catchie", "Punchinello little fellow", "ketchie bowlie", "duppy man a come," and the sweet memories!

Please don't just read this book and bask in your own memories, but call some children together and teach them three or more of these games. Tell them you're passing on a legacy, a legacy of lasting friend-ships—a legacy of beautiful, loving memories, and a legacy that's worth keeping for their children.

Obesity. Let's go outside on the play field and sweat while we laugh and talk, and run and play. Then straighten up and head back inside to study!

References

Henry, Fitzroy (2016, Aug. 3rd). Obesity in the Caribbean: A Case for Public Policies. https://www.omicsonline.org/open-access/obesity-in-the-caribbean-a-case-for-public-policies-2161-0509-1000194.php?aid=77372

Jamaican Patois Translator (2014). https://jamaicanize.com/translate?text=what

Jamaica Patwah (2013). http://jamaicanpatwah.com/dictionary/search?search_data=girl&search_btn.x=0&search_btn.y=0

Journeys: Caribbean Stories (2009). http://www.unlockingthearchives.rgs.org/themes/journeys/gallery/resource/?id=489

Murphy, Xavier (2004). Culture: *Games played by children in Jamaica* March 2004)
http://jamaicans.com/childgames/#ixzz4ojE4drvL

Murray, C,C. (2017) Skip To My Lou.
https://makingmusicfun.net/htm/f_mmf_music_library_songbook/skip-to-my-lou-history-and-lyrics.php

Glossary

An –	And
Bruk. –	Break
Bwoy –	Boy
Cannah –	Cannot
Dem –	Them
Dis –	This
Dodge –	Shifting from the thrown ball
Dung –	Going in a down ward direction
Gyal –	Girl
Fellow –	Fellow
Finga –	Finger
Inna –	In
Kinda –	Kind of
Mash –	To hurt by striking
Wah –	What

Blurb

As we observe the children today, constantly glued to a handheld machine while tiptoeing with their fingers continuously, smiling without a joke being heard, dancing without an audible sound for others to hear, not breaking a sweat, but tired most of the time, but not sleeping because of the ongoing night shifts of communication. It goes without saying they are being robbed of treasured experiences by always being stationed before a television box, a video game or the smart phones searching for amusement or entertainment.

While we had to be called to come inside, today's children are being told to go outside! From a psychological stand point this generation has been classified as the loneliest generation with so many 'likes', so many "friend requests" connected yet so disconnected. Friendships that can end by simply clicking a "block" button. People sending smiley faces while not smiling or saying "LOL", but silent in their rooms or sending beautiful hearts while having a broken heart; no wonder they can't sleep at night.

It is a travesty and something must be done. Hence, this book we hope will be a reminder to parents to spend some time teaching their children and the children in their communities and teachers setting aside a few minutes to teach their classes of what fun used to be. Fun being socially interactive without a phone in between. What "LOL" really looked and sounded like.

Are you ready? There's a brown girl in the ring. 1, 2, 3, Red light, let's go!

CPSIA information can be obtained
at www.ICGtesting.com
Printed in the USA
LVHW05s2245110518
576896LV00009B/281/P